CONTENTS

T0012058

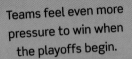

Teams feel even more pressure to win when the playoffs begin.

OPENING TIPOFF

THERE ARE 30 TEAMS IN THE NATIONAL BASKETBALL ASSOCIATION (NBA) AND 12 IN THE WOMEN'S NATIONAL BASKETBALL ASSOCIATION (WNBA). These teams are made up of some of the best basketball players in the world.

SPORTS' WILDEST UPSETS

PRO
BASKETBALL
UPSETS

MICKEY GILLIAM

Lerner Publications ◆ Minneapolis

Copyright © 2020 by Lerner Publishing Group, Inc.

All rights reserved. International copyright secured. No part of this book may be reproduced, stored in a retrieval system, or transmitted in any form or by any means—electronic, mechanical, photocopying, recording, or otherwise—without the prior written permission of Lerner Publishing Group, Inc., except for the inclusion of brief quotations in an acknowledged review.

Lerner Publications Company
An imprint of Lerner Publishing Group, Inc.
241 First Avenue North
Minneapolis, MN 55401 USA

For reading levels and more information, look up this title at www.lernerbooks.com.

Main body text set in Aptifer Sans LT Pro.
Typeface provided by Linotype AG.

Library of Congress Cataloging-in-Publication Data

Names: Gilliam, Mickey author. | Lerner Publishing Group, Inc.
Title: Pro basketball upsets / Mickey Gilliam
Description: Minneapolis : Lerner Publications, [2020] | Series: Sports' wildest upsets (Lerner Sports) | Audience: Ages: 7–11. | Audience: Grades: 4 to 6. | Includes bibliographical references and index.
Identifiers: LCCN 2019016677 (print) | LCCN 2019021884 (ebook) | ISBN 9781541583689 (eb pdf) | ISBN 9781541577169 (library binding : alk. paper) | ISBN 9781541589667 (paperback : alk. paper)
Subjects: LCSH: National Basketball Association—History—Juvenile literature. | Sports upsets—United States—History—Juvenile literature. | National Basketball Association—Miscellanea—Juvenile literature. | Basketball—United States—History—Juvenile literature. | Sports rivalries—United States—History—Juvenile literature.
Classification: LCC GV885.515.N37 (ebook) | LCC GV885.515.N37 G57 2020 (print) | DDC 796.323/640973—dc23

LC record available at https://lccn.loc.gov/2019016677

Manufactured in the United States of America
1 – CG – 12/31/19

Each pro season finishes with a playoff tournament for the best teams in the league. These best-of-three, best-of-five, or best-of-seven series can lead to amazing matchups. When great players go up against each other, anything can happen.

Because **underdog** teams have to win multiple games to win each playoff series, upsets are rare. That is why it is so exciting when they do happen. Any player or team can have a bad game or an injury that can lead to a surprising loss.

FACTS AT A GLANCE

- The Golden State Warriors played the Cleveland Cavaliers the 2016 NBA Finals. The Warriors had the best regular season record in NBA history and were favored to win the championship. The Cavaliers' victory came after they lost three of the first four games.

- Many believe the Detroit Shock's defeat of the Los Angeles Sparks for the 2003 title was the biggest upset in WNBA history. The Sparks were considered one of the greatest teams ever.

- The Miami Heat was made up of the NBA's best players in the 2010–2011 season. But the Dallas Mavericks, who had never won an NBA title, came to win and surprised everyone by beating the Heat.

DUMPING DALLAS

THE DALLAS MAVERICKS WERE IN A GOOD POSITION GOING INTO THE 2007 NBA PLAYOFFS. They were the top **seed** in the Western Conference. Their first-round opponents were the Golden State Warriors, who had barely made the playoffs.

The Dallas Mavericks won 67 games during the 2007 NBA season and had won the Western Conference the previous year.

Stephen Jackson's 33 points during Game 6 helped the Warriors upset the Mavericks.

But Golden State won three of the first four games. Dallas pushed ahead to win Game 5, and they needed to win Game 6 as well to stay alive. The Warriors were in trouble. Their star player, Baron Davis, had been on fire all series, averaging 25 points per game. But he had strained his hamstring. He couldn't play as aggressively as he usually did.

It was a close game at halftime. The Warriors were ahead by just two points. Then Golden State's Stephen Jackson stepped up, and everything fell apart for the Mavericks. Jackson hit four of his seven three-pointers during the third quarter. He continued to score during the fourth. The Warriors won 111–86 to take the series.

FINAL SERIES SCORE

WARRIORS	MAVERICKS
4	2

The Philadelphia 76ers won 52 games during the 1983–1984 season. The New Jersey Nets won 45.

DROPPING THE DOCTOR

SUPERSTAR JULIUS ERVING WAS NICKNAMED "DR. J." The talented forward led the Philadelphia 76ers to the NBA crown in 1983. The next year, they were supposed to roll in the Eastern Conference playoffs. The New Jersey Nets were expected to provide no problems in the first round. After all, they had never even won an NBA playoff game.

The Nets surprised almost everyone by winning the first two games. But the 76ers fought back and won the next two. It seemed like the tide had turned. Most believed Philadelphia would win Game 5 to take the series on its home court.

Albert King (55) took a shot over Erving during the 1984 Eastern Conference playoffs.

The Nets appeared doomed when they fell behind 90–83 with just seven minutes remaining. But they clawed their way back. Nets guard Micheal Ray Richardson tied the game with a foul shot with four minutes and 43 seconds left. The Nets took charge when Albert King stole the ball from Erving. King was fouled and hit both of his free throws. The Nets were up by five points. Erving and the other 76ers struggled the rest of the game. Richardson scored one last free throw to clinch the win for the Nets, which also secured the series victory.

Micheal Ray Richardson (*left*) was a big reason the Nets won against the 76ers.

"I can't even believe this feeling," Nets player Buck Williams said as his team celebrated. "There were so many who contributed. It's just wonderful."

Although the Nets went on to lose to the Milwaukee Bucks in the next round of the playoffs, they had pulled off one of the biggest upsets in NBA history.

FINAL SERIES SCORE

NETS | 76ERS
3 | 2

THE FEVER HEAT THINGS UP

THERE WAS NO REASON TO BELIEVE THE MINNESOTA LYNX WOULD LOSE TO THE INDIANA FEVER ON AUGUST 6, 2017. The Lynx were on a seven-game winning streak. The Fever had the second-worst record in the league. And they had lost five games in a row.

The Minnesota Lynx had a 20–2 record when they went up against the Indiana Fever in 2017.

Briann January was one of the best defenders in the WNBA, but she showed she could win games with her shooting too.

But the Fever stayed with the Lynx the entire game. The score was close up to the final minutes, thanks to Indiana forward Candice Dupree. She continued to make shot after shot.

Indiana was trailing by one point with 24 seconds left. Fever guard Marissa Coleman tried to put her team ahead with a three-pointer from the left corner. She was blocked. But the ball landed in the hands of teammate Erlana Larkins. She banked a shot with 8.2 seconds left to give the Fever the lead. Indiana's Briann January secured the win by hitting a free throw with less than a second left. The Fever had shocked everyone.

FINAL SCORE

FEVER	LYNX
84	**83**

TOO MUCH ELGIN

THE 1958-1959 ST. LOUIS HAWKS WERE NOT SUPPOSED TO STRUGGLE WITH THE MINNEAPOLIS LAKERS IN THE WESTERN DIVISION FINALS. The Hawks had finished first in their division with a 49–23 record. The Lakers finished 33–39.

Baylor went on to win the NBA Rookie of the Year Award for the 1958–1959 season.

St. Louis crushed Minneapolis in two of the first three games. But Minneapolis didn't make it easy the rest of the series. The Lakers won the next two games.

Game 6 could determine a conference champion. That is when Minneapolis forward Elgin Baylor took over. This superstar **rookie** exploded for 33 points.

Minneapolis owned a nine-point lead heading into the fourth quarter. They played tight defense to try and hold off St. Louis. The Lakers won by just two points.

COMINGS AND GOINGS

Minneapolis would not enjoy the Lakers for much longer. And St. Louis fans had just nine more years to watch their Hawks. The Lakers moved to Los Angeles in 1960. The Hawks moved to Atlanta in 1968.

FINAL SERIES SCORE

LAKERS	HAWKS
4	2

STUNNING SAN ANTONIO

THE MEMPHIS GRIZZLIES SEEMED DESTINED TO LOSE IN THE FIRST ROUND OF THE 2011 PLAYOFFS. They had lost every postseason game they had ever played. And their first-round foe was the top-seeded San Antonio Spurs.

The Memphis Grizzlies demonstrated strong defense against the San Antonio Spurs.

But Grizzlies power forward Zach Randolph sent a message to the Spurs from the start. He piled up 25 points and 14 rebounds in a Game 1 win. The Grizzlies played intense defense. Memphis led the series 3–2 after Game 5.

Randolph was on fire again in Game 6. With just over a minute remaining, Memphis was up 89–82. The Spurs tried to slow down Randolph's shooting streak by double-teaming him. But Randolph still hit a fallaway jumper. The Grizzlies scored eight more points in the final minute and pulled away for the victory.

FINAL SERIES SCORE

GRIZZLIES	SPURS
4	2

During his career, Dikembe Mutombo averaged three blocks per game.

THE NUGGETS CAME TO PLAY

SCORERS GET A LOT OF ATTENTION. Great defenders are sometimes ignored. But that was not the case for Denver Nuggets center Dikembe Mutombo in the 1994 playoffs. His team was a huge underdog against the top-seeded Seattle SuperSonics.

The 1994 playoffs marked the first time a number eight seed beat a number one seed.

Seattle won the first two games at home. The next two Denver victories altered the course of the series. Few people had given the Nuggets a chance to win.

A deciding Game 5 was played in Seattle. The game was close. Denver was ahead with less than a second left, but Seattle guard Kendall Gill tied the score with a layup. The game went into **overtime**. Mutombo had been swatting away shot after shot all game. Seattle's Shawn Kemp made one last scoring attempt, but Mutombo rejected his shot. With 18 seconds left, Denver's Robert Pack made two free throws to bring Denver's lead to four points. Then the clock ran out. The Nuggets walked away the winners.

FINAL SERIES SCORE

NUGGETS | SUPERSONICS

3 | 2

CLEVELAND'S COMEBACK

SUPERSTAR LEBRON JAMES VOWED TO WIN AN NBA CHAMPIONSHIP FOR HIS HOMETOWN TEAM, THE CLEVELAND CAVALIERS. He had his chance in the 2016 NBA Finals. Standing in his way were the Golden State Warriors. They had compiled a 73–9 record, the best in NBA history. Few gave the Cavs a chance to beat them.

LeBron James and the Cavs won Cleveland's first major sports championship in 52 years.

SPALDING

23

CURRY

Kyrie Irving averaged 27 points per game against the Warriors during the championship series.

The Warriors won three of the first four games. But then James and point guard Kyrie Irving went on a tear. They each scored 41 points in a Game 5 win. Cleveland won Game 6, too.

The championship came down to the fourth quarter of Game 7. It was tied 89–89 late in the game. James chased down Warriors guard Andre Iguodala and snuffed his layup at the rim to keep the score knotted. Then Irving nailed a three-pointer to win the game.

James had kept his promise. Cleveland fans went crazy. It was time to celebrate.

FINAL SERIES SCORE

CAVALIERS | WARRIORS
4 | **3**

The Detroit Shock had the best record in the WNBA in 2003, but they still had to beat the Los Angeles Sparks, who had won the championship the past two years.

THE SHOCK WIN IT ALL

THE DETROIT SHOCK HAD BEEN A BAD TEAM IN 2001 AND 2002. Before the 2003 season, they added forward Cheryl Ford and center Ruth Riley. The new talent helped the Shock earn a WNBA Finals spot. But the Los Angeles Sparks and their superstar center, Lisa Leslie, would be tough to beat.

Shock players celebrated their first WNBA championship after beating the Sparks.

The teams split the first two games. A league-record 22,076 fans filled The Palace in Auburn Hills, Michigan, for Game 3. The Shock led by four points with 25 seconds left. A Sparks three-pointer cut that lead to one point. But Ford and Deanna Nolan hit huge foul shots down the stretch. The Shock were able to capture the championship.

THE AMAZING LISA LESLIE

Sparks center Lisa Leslie ranks among the top WNBA players in career points, rebounds, and blocked shots. She was also the first WNBA player to dunk the ball in a game. It is no wonder that she won the league's Most Valuable Player (MVP) award three times.

FINAL SERIES SCORE

SHOCK	SPARKS
2	1

COOLING OFF THE HEAT

THE 2010–2011 MIAMI HEAT HAD LEBRON JAMES, DWYANE WADE, AND CHRIS BOSH, THREE OF THE NBA'S BEST PLAYERS. Miami expected an easy win against the Dallas Mavericks in the NBA Finals.

Dwyane Wade was one of the Miami Heat's top players in 2011.

Dirk Nowitzki held up the NBA championship trophy on June 12, 2011.

But Dallas showed that a united team could beat a collection of great individual talent. The Mavericks moved quickly on offense and played their defense well. Miami only focused on shooting the ball.

The Mavericks came to life in Game 4. Power forward Dirk Nowitzki drove for a layup with 14 seconds left in the game. With four seconds to go, Miami's Mike Miller tried for a three-pointer that would send the game into overtime. The ball missed the hoop. Dallas's victory tied the series. Then the Mavericks won the next two games, too. They had upset the star-studded Heat to win their first NBA title.

FINALS STREAK

LeBron James would not leave Miami until he won an NBA championship. His Heat won it in 2012 and 2013. They would lose in the finals the following year. Then James decided to return to Cleveland. In total, he played in eight straight NBA Finals from 2011 to 2018.

FINAL SERIES SCORE

MAVERICKS	HEAT
4	2

Fans thought Kobe Bryant and the Los Angeles Lakers would beat the Detroit Pistons in the 2004 NBA Finals.

DESTROYED BY DETROIT

THE LOS ANGELES LAKERS SEEMED UNBEATABLE HEADING INTO THE 2004 NBA FINALS. They had won three straight NBA titles from 2000 to 2002. The team featured center Shaquille O'Neal and **swingman** Kobe Bryant.

Ben Wallace celebrated after making a basket during Game 5.

Standing in the way of another championship were the Detroit Pistons. The Pistons had a lot of talent but no big-name players.

Yet throughout the series the Pistons played bruising defense that stopped the Lakers' best players. Detroit's Tayshaun Prince continually kept Bryant from getting open for shots.

Then in Game 5, the Pistons were crushing the Lakers by more than 20 points. Detroit's Richard Hamilton took a shot with minutes to go. Teammate Ben Wallace caught the ball after it bounced off the rim. He slammed it into the basket. Detroit rolled to the title with a 100–87 score. The Pistons showed that intensity and defense can win championships.

FINAL SERIES SCORE

PISTONS	LAKERS
4	1

OVERTIME

PRIOR TO 2003, THE FIRST ROUND OF THE NBA FINALS WERE BASED ON A BEST-OF-FIVE FORMAT, AND EVEN ONCE WERE BEST-OF-THREE. Since changing the first round to be best-of-seven, underdog teams have had less success in their quests for upsets. This makes the playoffs fairly predictable. **Favored** teams rarely lose three or four games to weaker opponents. But every so often, a team comes along to upset expectations and make things a whole lot more interesting.

Since the first NBA game in 1949, many amazing teams have played each other. Some of the league's most thrilling games have been shocking upsets.

Players can't help but celebrate together on the court after an unexpected win.

The focus in the NBA and WNBA has always been on their great players. How these players perform determines playoff wins and losses. Some players on weaker teams rise to the occasion when there are championships on the line. Sometimes the biggest superstars play poorly and let their teams down when the pressure's on. It's those surprises that can make the NBA and WNBA playoffs some of the most exciting games in all of sports.

SOURCE NOTE

11 *New York Times*, "Nets Stage Rally in Final Minutes to Eliminate 76ers," 14 May 2019, https://www.nytimes.com/1984/04/27/sports/nets-stage-rally-in-final-minutes-to-eliminate-76ers.html.

GLOSSARY

favored: expected to win a game or series

overtime: an extra session of play to determine a winner when a game is tied

playoffs: the series of games played to determine a league champion

rookie: a professional player in his or her first year in a league

seed: how a team is ranked based on regular season records to determine its playoff position

swingman: a player who can play a guard or forward position

underdog: the team expected to lose a game or series

FURTHER INFORMATION

Fishman, Jon M. *Breanna Stewart*. Minneapolis: Lerner Publications, 2019.

Jr. NBA
https://jr.nba.com

Latta, Ivory and Smith, Charles R. *Despite the Height*. Charlotte, NC: Warren Publishing, 2017.

NBA Math Hoops
http://www.nbamathhoops.org/about.php

Sports Illustrated Kids: Basketball
https://www.sikids.com/basketball

Whiting, Jim. *Golden State Warriors*. Mankato, MN: Creative Paperbacks, 2018.

INDEX

PHOTO ACKNOWLEDGMENTS

The images in this book are used with the permission of: © Rob Carr/Getty Images Sport/Getty Images, p. 4; © Jed Jacobsohn/Getty Images Sport/Getty Images, pp. 6, 7; © Focus on Sport/Getty Images Sport/Getty Images, pp. 8, 9, 10, 11; © Jeffrey Brown/Icon Sportswire/Getty Images, pp. 12, 13; © Bettmann/Getty Images, pp. 14, 15; © Andy Lyons/Getty Images Sport/Sport, pp. 16, 21; © Thearon W. Henderson/Getty Images Sport/Getty Images, p. 17; © Gary Stewart/AP Images, pp. 18, 19; © Beck Diefenbach/AFP/Getty Images, p. 20; © Lisa Blumenfeld/Getty Images Sport/Getty Images, p. 22; © Tom Pidgeon/Getty Images Sport/Getty Images, p. 23; © Ronald Martinez/Getty Images Sport/Getty Images, p. 24; © Mark Ralston/AFP/Getty Images Sport, p. 25; © Jeff Haynes/AFP/Getty Images, p. 26; © Elsa/Getty Images Sport/Getty Images, p. 27; © Stan Honda/AFP/Getty Images, p. 28; © Jonathan Daniel/Getty Images Sport/Getty Images, p. 29.

Front cover: © Jed Jacobsohn/Getty Images Sport/Getty Images, top left; © Andy Lyons/Getty Images Sport/Getty Images, top right; © Beck Diefenbach/AFP/Getty Images, bottom.